CAMBRIDGE

A2
KEY 2

WITHOUT ANSWERS

AUTHENTIC PRACTICE TESTS

Cambridge University Press
www.cambridge.org/elt

Cambridge Assessment English
www.cambridgeenglish.org

Information on this title: www.cambridge.org/9781108748780

© Cambridge University Press and Cambridge Assessment 2020

It is normally necessary for written permission for copying to be obtained
in advance from a publisher. The sample answer sheets at the back of this
book are designed to be copied and distributed in class.
The normal requirements are waived here and it is not necessary to write to
Cambridge University Press for permission for an individual teacher to make copies
for use within his or her own classroom. Only those pages that carry the wording
'© Cambridge Assessment 2020 Photocopiable' may be copied.

First published 2020

20 19 18 17 16 15 14 13 12 11 10 9 8 7 6 5 4 3 2

Printed in Great Britain by Ashford Colour Ltd.

A catalogue record for this publication is available from the British Library

ISBN 978-1-108-78158-9 A2 Key 2 Student's Book with answers with Audio
ISBN 978-1-108-74878-0 A2 Key 2 Student's Book without answers

The publishers have no responsibility for the persistence or accuracy of URLs
for external or third-party internet websites referred to in this publication, and
do not guarantee that any content on such websites is, or will remain, accurate
or appropriate. Information regarding prices, travel timetables, and other factual
information given in this work is correct at the time of first printing but the
publishers do not guarantee the accuracy of such information thereafter.

Contents

Contents

Introduction

Prepare for the exam with practice tests from Cambridge

Inside you'll find four authentic examination papers from Cambridge Assessment English. They are the perfect way to practise – EXACTLY like the real exam.

Why are they unique?

All our authentic practice tests go through the same design process as the *A2 Key* exam. We check every single part of our practice tests with real students under exam conditions, to make sure we give you the most authentic experience possible.

Students can practise these tests on their own or with the help of a teacher to familiarise themselves with the exam format, understand the scoring system and practise exam technique.

Cambridge English Qualifications	CEFR Level	UK National Qualifications Framework Level
C2 Proficiency	C2	3
C1 Advanced	C1	2
B2 First	B2	1
B1 Preliminary	B1	Entry 3
A2 Key	A2	Entry 2

Further information

The information contained in this practice book is designed to be an overview of the exam. For a full description of all of the above exams, including information about task types, testing focus and preparation, please see the relevant handbooks which can be obtained from the Cambridge Assessment English website at: **cambridgeenglish.org**.

The structure of *A2 Key*: an overview

The *Cambridge English Qualifications A2 Key* examination consists of three papers:

Reading and Writing: 60 minutes

Candidates need to be able to understand simple written information such as signs and newspapers, and produce simple written English.

Listening: 30 minutes approximately

Candidates need to show they can follow and understand a range of spoken materials such as announcements, when people speak reasonably slowly.

Speaking: 8–10 minutes

Candidates take the Speaking test with another candidate or in a group of three. They are tested on their ability to take part in different types of interaction: with the examiner, with the other candidate and by themselves.

	Overall length	Number of tasks/ parts	Number of items
Reading and Writing	60 mins	7	32
Listening	approx. 30 mins	5	25
Speaking	8–10 mins	2	–
Total	approx. 1 hour 40 mins		

Grading

All candidates receive a Statement of Results and candidates whose performance ranges between CEFR Levels A1 and B1 (Cambridge English Scale scores of 100–150) also receive a certificate.

- Candidates who achieve **Grade A** (Cambridge English Scale scores of 140–150) receive the Key English Test certificate stating that they demonstrated ability at Level B1.
- Candidates who achieve **Grade B** or **C** (Cambridge English Scale scores of 120–139) receive the Key English Test certificate at Level A2.
- Candidates whose performance is below A2 level, but falls within **Level A1** (Cambridge English Scale scores of 100–119), receive a Cambridge English certificate stating that they have demonstrated ability at Level A1.

For further information on grading and results, go to the website (see page 5 for details).

Speaking: an overview for candidates

The Speaking test lasts 8–10 minutes. You will take the test with another candidate. There are two examiners but only one of them will talk to you. The examiner will ask you questions and ask you to talk to the other candidate.

Part 1 (3–4 minutes)
The examiner will ask you and your partner some questions. These questions will be about your daily life, interests, likes and dislikes. For example, you may have to speak about your school, hobbies or home town.

Part 2 (5–6 minutes)
You and your partner will speak to each other. The examiner will give you a card with some illustrations on it. You will then discuss the activities, things or places illustrated on the card with your partner. The examiner will then ask you and your partner some individual questions about the illustrations on the card.

Test 1

READING AND WRITING (60 minutes)

PART 1

QUESTIONS 1–6

For each question, choose the correct answer.

1

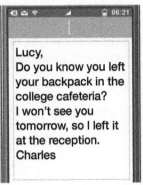

Lucy,
Do you know you left your backpack in the college cafeteria?
I won't see you tomorrow, so I left it at the reception.
Charles

  A   Charles is asking Lucy where he should leave her backpack.

  B   Charles is checking if Lucy has lost her backpack.

  C   Charles is letting Lucy know where her backpack is.

2

> *History tour:*
>
> Nottingham Castle
> Daily (12.00)
>
> Please email guide to book free place
>
> historywalk@mail.com

  A   You have to go to the castle to book the walking tour.

  B   You should send an email to find out when the next walking tour is.

  C   You need to contact the guide before you can go on the walking tour.

3

Hannah,
I'm booking the cinema tickets online. The 3 p.m. show's full, but there are seats for 5.30 p.m. and 8 p.m. There's a discount before 6 p.m.
Lydia

Lydia is telling Hannah that

  A   they'll pay less to see the film at 5.30 p.m.

  B   they need to book cinema tickets by 3 p.m.

  C   it's not possible for them to see the film at 8 p.m.

4

Steve,
Are you still at work?
I'm nearly finished,
but I won't be able to
get to the restaurant
till after 7.30. Sorry.
Andy

Why did Andy write this text?

A   to suggest meeting Steve at a different restaurant

B   to explain to Steve that he will be late

C   to tell Steve why he can't meet him

5

Henry,
Do you know which
restaurant we're
going to tonight? Ella
wants to join us. Is
that OK? I think she
knows everyone.
Suzy

What is Suzy doing?

A   asking Henry if she can bring an extra person to the restaurant tonight

B   telling Henry about the restaurant she has chosen for tonight

C   checking who is going to be at the restaurant tonight

6

NOTICES

Our dentists are busy.
Please arrive five minutes
before your appointment.
If you miss your appointment,
you'll need to make one for
another day.

People who are late

A   will have to see a different dentist.

B   won't see their dentist that day.

C   must wait until a dentist is free to see them.

PART 2

QUESTIONS 7–13

For each question, choose the correct answer.

		Angus	Frank	Zac
7	Who needed help with the internet on his first day?	A	B	C
8	Who felt sad when his parents went home?	A	B	C
9	Who took something to university to help him make friends?	A	B	C
10	Who started university later than other students?	A	B	C
11	Who is still friends with someone he met on his first day at university?	A	B	C
12	Who thinks he has changed since he started university?	A	B	C
13	Who met other new students online before starting university?	A	B	C

Making friends at university

Angus

My university has an internet group for new students, which I joined before I went. One person on there said that on her sister's first day, she brought sweets from home to offer to everyone she met, as a way to start a conversation. I thought that was a good idea, so I did the same. It worked, but in fact, the really good friends I have now are all people I met a few weeks later.

Frank

I live at my university, and Mum and Dad drove me here on my first day. After they left, I felt terrible. I sat alone looking at photos of friends from home. But later, I went to a talk about all the university clubs, and I really enjoyed it. Clubs are a great way to meet people, and if you're going to university, you should join some. They helped me a lot. Before I came to university, I was a quiet person, but these days I can talk to people more easily.

Zac

I was away on holiday with my parents for the first week of my university course, so I missed all of the activities where people make friends. On that first morning, I couldn't get online, so I went looking for someone who knew what to do. The student I found got my wi-fi working and is now my best friend. I've also met lots of people because of him. Mum and Dad say I've grown up since I started university, but I'm not sure.

PART 3

QUESTIONS 14–18

For each question, choose the correct answer.

Amazing balloon flight

Tom Morgan flew 25 kilometres across South Africa using only 100 party balloons.

Tom Morgan is a British man who started a club planning adventures for people. His idea is to give people some danger in their lives, as he thinks we don't have enough of that these days. The adventures he plans include races across various countries using unusual types of transport.

Last year Tom went to Africa for a crazy adventure with some friends. The plan was to tie 100 party balloons to a chair Tom was sitting in, and make it fly into the air. Tom's not the first person to do this. Jonathan Trappe from the USA has done it, but it was an article in an adventure magazine that made Tom want to try it.

Tom chose the country of Botswana for his adventure because it has lots of empty space and isn't near the sea. However, the weather was so windy there that they lost lots of balloons, so they went to South Africa instead. This time, the flight was a great success.

Tom says the views from 2,400 metres up were amazing, and remembers how quiet it was. However, he spent most of the time worrying about what to do if he flew too high and how to get back down.

One reason Tom did his balloon flight was to check if it's possible to fly using party balloons. Now he knows it is, he's planning the first party balloon air race in Africa. He hopes lots of his club members will enter.

---

14   Why did Tom start his adventure club?

   A   He thinks everyone should travel more.

   B   He believes that modern life is too safe.

   C   He wants to meet people who like adventures.

15   Tom got the idea for flying with balloons from

   A   a man from the USA.

   B   his friends.

   C   a magazine article.

16   Tom wasn't able to fly in Botswana because

   A   he needed more space.

   B   the weather was bad.

   C   he wanted to be nearer to the sea.

17   How did Tom feel during the flight?

   A   pleased that there was no noise

   B   surprised to have good views

   C   scared about what might happen

18   What is Tom working on at the moment?

   A   starting a new type of balloon race

   B   winning a balloon competition

   C   flying further with balloons

PART 4

QUESTIONS 19–24

For each question, choose the correct answer.

The coldest place to live

Oymyakon is a village in a part of Russia called Yakutia. During the winter, the days are **(19)** .... , and temperatures can go as **(20)** .... as -68°C. There are colder places in the world, such as Antarctica, but people only **(21)** .... there for a few weeks. Oymyakon is the coldest place where people live all the time.

A lot of things don't work normally in Oymyakon because it's so cold. For example, if a car is **(22)** .... outside, the engine will not start again, so people keep cars in heated garages. It is also very difficult to **(23)** .... plants for food when it is so cold, so people in Oymyakon mostly eat meat. In some countries, schools close when it's very cold, but that only **(24)** .... in Oymyakon if it's colder than -52°C.

19	**A**	early	**B**	short	**C**	quick
20	**A**	deep	**B**	small	**C**	low
21	**A**	stay	**B**	spend	**C**	come
22	**A**	gone	**B**	waited	**C**	left
23	**A**	make	**B**	put	**C**	grow
24	**A**	happens	**B**	passes	**C**	arrives

PART 5

QUESTIONS 25–30

For each question, write the correct answer.
Write **ONE** word for each gap.

Example:

0	*are*

From:	Sylvia
To:	Felix

I'm so glad we **(0)** .... doing our history project together! **(25)** .... you think the college library will have some useful books about local history? **(26)** .... don't we meet there tomorrow? Remember we've only got three weeks before we have **(27)** .... give the project to the teacher.

From:	Felix
To:	Sylvia

Don't worry! **(28)** .... we work really hard, then our project will be brilliant! Yes, let's meet at the college library. I'm sure we'll find lots **(29)** .... interesting books there. I'm afraid I'm busy tomorrow, **(30)** .... I'm free on Friday. Can you meet me then?

PART 6

QUESTION 31

You visited a city in your country last weekend.
Write an email to your English friend, Alex.

In your email:

• say which city you visited

• tell Alex how you travelled there

• explain what you did in the city.

Write **25 words** or more.

Write the email on your answer sheet.

PART 7

QUESTION 32

Look at the three pictures.
Write the story shown in the pictures.
Write **35 words** or more.

Write the story on your answer sheet.

LISTENING (approximately 30 minutes)

PART 1

QUESTIONS 1–5

For each question, choose the correct answer.

---

1 What temperature will the woman use to cook the cake?

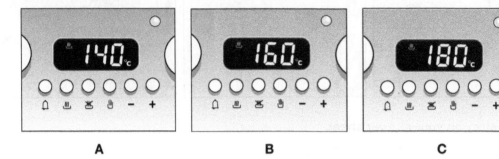

A   B   C

2 What did Clara hurt when she played tennis?

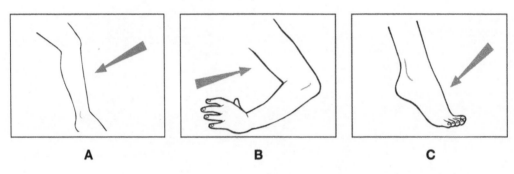

A   B   C

3 Which photo did the man take?

A   B   C

4 Which was the woman's favourite present?

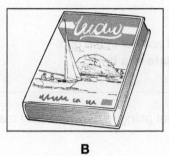

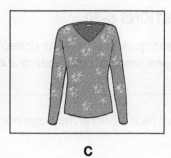

A   B   C

5 What did Tom lose?

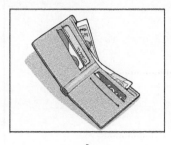

A   B   C

PART 2

QUESTIONS 6–10

For each question, write the correct answer in the gap.
Write **one word** or a **number** or a **date** or a **time**.

You will hear a phone message about going to play a hockey match.

Hockey match

Name of other team: Tigers

Day: (6) ....

Name of village: (7) ....

Travel to village by: (8) ....

Take: (9) ....

Time match begins: (10) ....

PART 3

QUESTIONS 11–15

For each question, choose the correct answer.

You will hear Sue talking to her friend Peter about a restaurant she went to.

11 Why didn't Peter go to the restaurant with Sue?

    A   He had to do some work.

    B   He was too ill.

    C   He forgot to go.

12 How long has the restaurant been open?

    A   one year

    B   two years

    C   five years

13 What did Sue and her friends eat at the restaurant?

    A   steak

    B   pizza

    C   pasta

14 What nationality is the chef at the restaurant?

    A   American

    B   Spanish

    C   Italian

15 What does Peter say about his plans to go to the restaurant?

    A   It doesn't matter which day he goes.

    B   He's afraid the restaurant will be too crowded.

    C   He'd like Sue's advice about the dishes.

PART 4

QUESTIONS 16–20

For each question, choose the correct answer.

---

16   You will hear a man and a woman talking about going shopping.
What will they buy?

   A   something to eat

   B   something to wear

   C   something to read

17   You will hear a woman leaving a message for a friend.
Why is the woman phoning her friend?

   A   to change their plans

   B   to ask to borrow something

   C   to invite her for a meal

18   You will hear a man telling his sister about meeting someone yesterday.
Who did he see in town?

   A   a colleague

   B   a neighbour

   C   an old school friend

19   You will hear two friends making plans for the day.
Where do they decide to go?

   A   to the forest

   B   to the river

   C   to the beach

20   You will hear a city tour guide giving a talk.
Why is the museum closed now?

   A   A special guest is visiting it.

   B   Today is a national holiday.

   C   They are painting it.

PART 5

QUESTIONS 21–25

For each question, choose the correct answer.

You will hear Susan talking to a friend about the sports she does.
Which sport does she do with each person now?

Example:

0	Elias	**H**

People

21 Daniel

22 Amira

23 Kelly

24 Ryan

25 Valerie

Sports

A badminton

B fishing

C football

D golf

E skateboarding

F swimming

G tennis

H volleyball

You now have 6 minutes to write your answers on the answer sheet.

23

Test 2

READING AND WRITING (60 minutes)

PART 1

QUESTIONS 1–6

For each question, choose the correct answer.

1

NOTICES

**Woodside Train Station
Gardening Group**

Help make our platforms
beautiful!
If you're over 16 and know how
to grow plants and flowers,
call Louise (046289432)

Contact Louise if you want to

A improve the way the station looks.

B learn how to make a nice garden.

C travel to see some beautiful gardens.

2

File Edit Tools View Message Help
To: Chloe
From: Mrs Jones

Thanks for your idea for
the school project, but
someone is already doing
'Local Transport'. What
about 'Fashion'? There's
lots of information online.

A Mrs Jones wants Chloe to do a different subject for her project.

B Mrs Jones thinks Chloe's idea for the project is too difficult.

C Mrs Jones wants Chloe to do her project with someone else.

3

Kate,
I'll meet you at the
gym this afternoon
instead of at the bus
stop. I have to go
into town first.
Jana

A Jana's not sure which bus to catch to town this afternoon.

B It's not possible for Jana to go to the gym today.

C Kate will not see Jana at the bus stop later today.

4

WANTED

Actors for the new play
No experience needed
For more information
contact Ben

020 693 417

A   Ben wants to talk to people who have ideas for a new play.

B   You can get further details about the play by talking to Ben.

C   Ben is only interested in talking to people who have acted before.

5

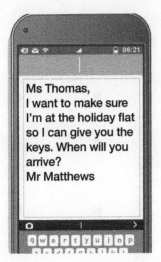

Ms Thomas,
I want to make sure I'm at the holiday flat so I can give you the keys. When will you arrive?
Mr Matthews

What is Mr Matthews doing in this message?

A   asking what time he can meet Ms Thomas

B   letting Ms Thomas know where she'll find the keys

C   telling Ms Thomas that she can book the holiday flat

6

Kay,
The hall's booked for the college party and the invitations are ready. We just need a band. Do you know a good one?
Ria

Ria wants Kay's help with

A   inviting guests to the party.

B   getting music for the party.

C   finding a hall for the party.

PART 2

QUESTIONS 7–13

For each question, choose the correct answer.

		Rafa	Dan	Claudio
7	Who thinks one of the actors in his favourite film is better than another?	A	B	C
8	Who says his favourite film wasn't very successful at the cinema?	A	B	C
9	Who feels sad at the end of his favourite film?	A	B	C
10	Who explains where he first saw his favourite film?	A	B	C
11	Who explains what happens in his favourite film?	A	B	C
12	Who says his favourite film is a true story?	A	B	C
13	Who tries to see his favourite film every twelve months?	A	B	C

My favourite film

Rafa

The first time I saw *Silver River* was at my friend's house. It's the story of two families, which didn't sound very interesting to me, but actually I loved it. I saw it again last week, and I enjoyed it just as much. The actors are good and so is the story, but what I really love is the music – it's brilliant. When the film first came out, not many people went to see it, but it's a lot more popular now.

Dan

For me, *Forest Path* is the best film ever. It's about a musician who leaves his home in Mexico and goes looking for adventure. He travels around the country for a year, playing his guitar everywhere he goes. At the end of the film, he meets the woman who becomes his wife. This actually happened in real life many years ago, which I didn't know when I first saw it. The acting is very good, especially the woman – she has more acting experience than the man.

Claudio

I can't remember when or where I first saw *Black Hole*, but it's a film I like to watch at least once a year. It's about travelling through space, and to me the acting and the story are not important – it's the way it's filmed. It's like a dream and nothing seems real. At the time, this was a new way of making films and since then lots of people have copied the idea. The music is very beautiful, and the final moments always make me cry.

PART 3

QUESTIONS 14–18

For each question, choose the correct answer.

My life as a tour guide

Kerri Benson talks about the job she loves.

I was looking for work after I finished university when a friend of mine told me about her fantastic job as a tour guide. She was able to help me get a job with her company and now, every two weeks, a driver and I take a group of tourists across five European countries by coach.

Before each tour, the driver takes the coach from the city where the last tour finished to the one where the next tour starts, but I fly there. When I get to the hotel, I make sure I have all the right forms and visas for the new group of tourists. It's important that I have everything.

I'm friendly towards the tourists, but I always remember that they're my customers. There's no boss to help with problems, which can be difficult, but I love it when our coach is full of happy people, excited about their trip.

The company has a website for all of the tour guides to share information. Some post information about journey times, but that changes so quickly it's not very useful. My posts are usually about interesting museums, castles and things like that. And I read other guides' ideas for restaurants to take customers to.

This is a job for people who enjoy travelling and planning. If you're thinking of doing it, go on a tour as a customer first. It's a good way to see what guides do. Just remember that guides don't get paid much. For me, that's not a problem, but it might be for some people.

---

14   What does Kerri say about becoming a tour guide?

    A   She took the job because she couldn't find anything better.

    B   She needed a job that she could do in her university holidays.

    C   She got the job because she knew someone at the company.

15   Before each tour, Kerri

    A   drives to the place where the tour will start.

    B   checks that she has the documents she needs.

    C   makes sure that enough hotel rooms are booked.

16   What does Kerri enjoy about her job?

    A   seeing people having a good holiday

    B   meeting people who become friends

    C   helping people with problems

17   Kerri gives other tour guides information about

    A   where to eat.

    B   places to visit.

    C   traffic problems.

18   What advice does Kerri have for people who want to do her job?

    A   Take a tour to see if you like it.

    B   Talk to people who are already guides.

    C   Find a company that pays guides well.

PART 4

QUESTIONS 19–24

For each question, choose the correct answer.

The Nobel Prize

Every year, in October, a small number of very special people get a very important phone call. It is a call which can change the rest of their careers and almost **(19)** .... they become famous. That is because this is the phone call **(20)** .... them they have won a Nobel Prize.

There are five Nobel Prizes in **(21)** .... , three of which are given to scientists. The prize is international and scientists from around the world have **(22)** .... one. There are several **(23)** .... why winning a Nobel Prize is important. First of all, it is a lot of money – about $1.1 million. **(24)** .... , the most important thing about a Nobel Prize is that the scientist's work gets a lot of attention.

19	**A**	early	**B**	immediately	**C**	exactly
20	**A**	speaking	**B**	telling	**C**	explaining
21	**A**	part	**B**	variety	**C**	total
22	**A**	received	**B**	taken	**C**	included
23	**A**	instructions	**B**	reasons	**C**	differences
24	**A**	Instead	**B**	However	**C**	Especially

PART 5

QUESTIONS 25–30

For each question, write the correct answer.
Write **ONE** word for each gap.

Example:

0	are

From:	Erin
To:	Lara

How **(0)** .... you? I moved into a new house last month. It's a lot bigger **(25)** ....

my old house, and **(26)** .... is a big garden at the back. I can't wait **(27)** .... grow

some vegetables in it!

It's taken me and my parents **(28)** .... long time to paint all the rooms, but we're going

to finish them soon. So **(29)** .... you like to come and stay with me next weekend? If

the weather's good, Mum says we can have a barbecue. I can show **(30)** .... some

interesting places in my town too.

Write soon!

PART 6

QUESTION 31

Read the email from your English friend, Chris.

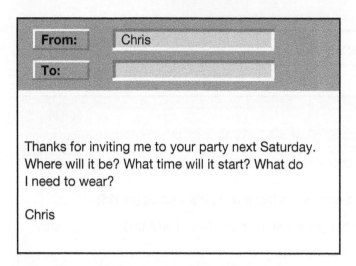

Thanks for inviting me to your party next Saturday. Where will it be? What time will it start? What do I need to wear?

Chris

Write an email to Chris and answer the questions.
Write **25 words** or more.

Write the email on your answer sheet.

PART 7

QUESTION 32

Look at the three pictures.
Write the story shown in the pictures.
Write **35 words** or more.

Write the story on your answer sheet.

LISTENING (approximately 30 minutes)

PART 1

QUESTIONS 1–5

For each question, choose the correct answer.

---

1 How did Richard travel from the airport?

A   B   C

2 What is next to the woman's new flat?

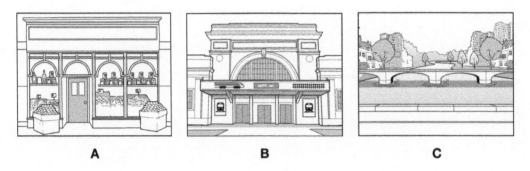

A   B   C

3 What job does the man do?

A   B   C

4   Which T-shirt does the girl decide to buy?

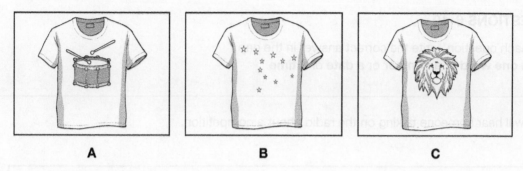

A   B   C

5   Where are the car keys?

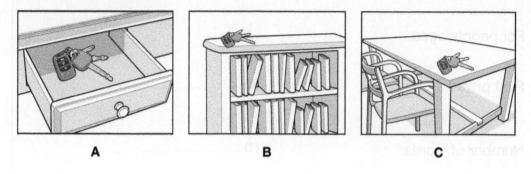

A   B   C

PART 2

QUESTIONS 6–10

For each question, write the correct answer in the gap.
Write **one word** or a **number** or a **date** or a **time**.

You will hear someone talking on the radio about a competition.

Short story competition

For people aged: 16

First prize: **(6)** ....

Number of words: **(7)** ....

Story must include the word: **(8)** ....

Last date to send story: **(9)** ....

Upload to: WWW.**(10)** .... .com

PART 3

QUESTIONS 11–15

For each question, choose the correct answer.

You will hear a brother and sister, Ben and Lily, talking about their mother's birthday.

11 When will they go shopping for a present?

    A   tomorrow morning

    B   tomorrow afternoon

    C   tomorrow evening

12 Where do they decide to go for some earrings?

    A   a department store

    B   the market

    C   a jewellery shop

13 Ben thinks that on their mum's birthday they should

    A   have a party for her.

    B   take her out for a meal.

    C   go to the park for a barbecue.

14 How does Lily feel about inviting their mum's best friend?

    A   excited about seeing her

    B   worried she will not come

    C   sure their mum will like the idea

15 What sort of drink will Ben make for their mum's birthday?

    A   banana and cream

    B   lemon and orange

    C   melon and honey

PART 4

QUESTIONS 16–20

For each question, choose the correct answer.

___

16 You will hear a woman telling her friend about a holiday.
   What was the only thing she liked about her holiday?

   A where she stayed

   B a place she ate at

   C an activity she did

17 You will hear a woman talking to her husband about a problem.
   Why is the woman upset?

   A Her car needs repairing.

   B She has lost some money.

   C Someone stole her bicycle.

18 You will hear an advertisement on the radio.
   What's the main reason for the advertisement?

   A to give details about a sale

   B to give information about a special day

   C to tell people about new equipment

19 You will hear a boy talking with his mother about one of his paintings.
   What doesn't the boy like about his painting?

   A its size

   B its colours

   C its subject

20 You will hear a girl talking to her father about a sports blog.
   What reason does the girl give for liking the blog?

   A the sports advice

   B the online competitions

   C the information about sports stars

PART 5

QUESTIONS 21–25

For each question, choose the correct answer.

You will hear a woman talking to her teenage son about putting some things in the right places in their new house.
Where should her son put each thing?

Example:

0	magazine	H

Things				**Places**	
21	bowl			A	bathroom
				B	bedroom
22	lamp			C	dining room
23	box			D	garden
				E	hall
24	clock			F	kitchen
25	chair			G	living room
				H	stairs

You now have 6 minutes to write your answers on the answer sheet.

Test 3

READING AND WRITING (60 minutes)

PART 1

QUESTIONS 1–6

For each question, choose the correct answer.

1

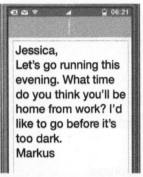

Jessica,
Let's go running this evening. What time do you think you'll be home from work? I'd like to go before it's too dark.
Markus

A Markus is letting Jessica know what time he's going running tonight.

B Markus is asking Jessica if she has arrived home from work yet.

C Markus is checking if Jessica will be home early enough to go running.

2

City Arts Centre

Do you belong to our theatre group? Has acting changed your life? Tell us and we'll put your story on our website.

What does the Arts Centre want to do?

A start a new theatre group

B share members' experiences online

C find out what people think of their website

3

Marcia,
Sorry to hear you're not very well. Do you need me to get you anything at the shops? Maybe some medicine or fruit?
Glenn

Why has Glenn sent Marcia this message?

A to make sure she has taken her medicine

B to ask if she is feeling better

C to find out how he can help

4

File Edit Tools View Message Help

To: Harry
From: Ollie

My tennis club on Saturday was really good fun. Why don't you become a member too? You'll love it.

Ollie has emailed Harry

A   to see if he wants to join the tennis club.

B   to ask him for his opinion of the tennis club.

C   to find out which tennis club he belongs to.

5

Fun quiz competition

22nd March 9 p.m.

£10 to enter

Book soon, almost full!

Cash prizes

A   Hurry if you would like to take part in the quiz.

B   The winner of the quiz will get a prize of £10.

C   The quiz will finish by 9 p.m. on 22nd March.

6

Stefan,
I've checked online and there's a problem with the buses. Mum's driving me to school. Shall we pick you up on the way?
Mark

Mark has texted Stefan

A   to tell him to look online.

B   to ask about the traffic.

C   to offer him a lift.

PART 2

QUESTIONS 7–13

For each question, choose the correct answer.

		Hillside	Green Farm	Castletown
7	Which campsite is good for people who enjoy outdoor sports?	A	B	C
8	Which campsite is near the sea?	A	B	C
9	Which campsite has its own shop?	A	B	C
10	Which campsite can be difficult to find?	A	B	C
11	Which campsite has friendly staff?	A	B	C
12	Which campsite is good for people with young children?	A	B	C
13	Which campsite can be noisy at night?	A	B	C

Three great campsites to visit

Hillside

This campsite is quite near a main road, so it's easy to find. You can camp there anytime you like, even in winter, which is why most of the things to do are inside – the pool, the games room and the café. Families will enjoy it here, as the pool is very safe and there's a lovely playground. It's also very quiet at night – there's no disco or noisy groups of campers. The staff are good, but they should try to be more friendly.

Green Farm

You can easily get lost on the way to Green Farm if you don't know where you're going. There are lots of activities for adults and teenagers to do on the campsite, including a golf course and a lake where you can go fishing and sailing. If you're interested in surfing, you should probably choose a different campsite, as Green Farm is quite a long way from the sea. If you need to buy food, there's a small supermarket next to the office.

Castletown

Castletown is right next to a village, and just a short walk from a beach. It's open from April to October. It's probably not the best place for older people or young children, as there's a disco in the village that plays loud music until quite late. The shops in the village are very useful, as there aren't any on the campsite. Campsite staff can help you with any problems or questions, and are always smiling and chatting with visitors.

PART 3

QUESTIONS 14–18

For each question, choose the correct answer.

An exciting hobby

Tanya Phillips explains why she's crazy about motorbikes.

I started riding a motorbike when I was 18. I was living in Edinburgh at the time, and I was using the bus to get to work, which I hated. I thought about learning to drive, but cars are expensive, so I bought a motorbike. I was the first of my friends to get one.

Over the next 5 years, I only used my motorbike in the city. Then a friend invited me on a motorbike ride through the Australian desert. It was amazing, and when I got home, I bought an adventure motorbike and started riding in wild places like forests in my free time.

Before any big ride, I make sure I know exactly where I'm going. I don't like asking for help, so I take maps and check the weather. Then when I'm riding, I can just forget about everything except me and the bike. That's what I like best.

I'm not afraid of riding in unusual places. I went to Iceland in the middle of winter. It was dark most of the day, so I had to be really careful and stay on the roads. I'd like to go again in summer when there's more light and then I can go on the smaller paths.

This year, I did my first 24-hour adventure motorbike race – across the African desert. It was really difficult, and when I finished all I wanted to do was sleep. But then I found out I was the winner – I couldn't believe it! I can't wait to enter next year's race.

---

14   Tanya first began riding a motorbike because

    A   she didn't like driving a car in Edinburgh.

    B   her friends told her it was a good idea.

    C   she wanted a better way to travel to her job.

15   When did riding a motorbike become Tanya's hobby?

    A   after a trip

    B   after riding through a forest

    C   after meeting someone in Australia

16   What's Tanya's favourite thing about riding a motorbike?

    A   She can spend time alone.

    B   She can look at the countryside.

    C   She can stop thinking about other things.

17   If Tanya goes to Iceland again,

    A   she'll go to another part of the country.

    B   she'll go at a different time of year.

    C   she'll spend more time there.

18   After her first motorbike race, Tanya was surprised by

    A   how well she did.

    B   how tired she felt.

    C   how difficult the race was.

PART 4

QUESTIONS 19–24

For each question, choose the correct answer.

David Bowie

The English pop star David Bowie was born David Robert Jones on 8th January, 1947. He was **(19)** .... in music from an early age and began playing in bands when he was still a teenager. When he was 18, he changed his name to David Bowie as there was another musician in the US **(20)** .... was also called David Jones.

David Bowie's song 'Space Oddity' was his first big hit, and it was popular around the world. He **(21)** .... later that he got the **(22)** .... for the song while he was watching a film called *2001: A Space Odyssey*.

Through his career, David Bowie often changed the **(23)** .... he looked and the kind of music he played. His final album was called 'Blackstar' and it became **(24)** .... to his fans on his 69th birthday. This was just two days before he died on 10th January, 2016.

19	A	interested	B	pleased	C	special
20	A	which	B	where	C	who
21	A	told	B	explained	C	talked
22	A	idea	B	experience	C	reason
23	A	thing	B	way	C	type
24	A	able	B	possible	C	available

PART 5

QUESTIONS 25–30

For each question, write the correct answer.
Write **ONE** word for each gap.

Example:

0	to

From:	Ellie
To:	Leah

I'm really pleased you're coming **(0)** .... stay at my house next week. We haven't seen each other for such **(25)** .... long time!

(26) .... are lots of things to do **(27)** .... my town, so I'm sure we'll have lots of fun. We can visit the museum and the theatre. And how about going shopping too? Our new shopping centre has some really great shops, and they're cheaper **(28)** .... the ones in the city.

I'll meet you at the airport on Saturday. **(29)** .... time does your flight arrive? Please let **(30)** .... know and I'll make a plan. I can't wait to see you again!

PART 6

QUESTION 31

Read the email from your English friend, Jan.

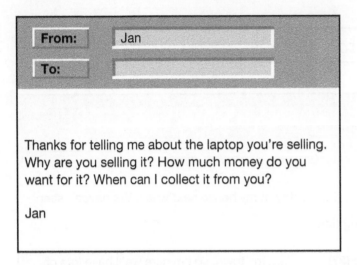

From: Jan

To:

Thanks for telling me about the laptop you're selling. Why are you selling it? How much money do you want for it? When can I collect it from you?

Jan

Write an email to Jan and answer the questions.
Write **25 words** or more.

Write the email on your answer sheet.

PART 7

QUESTION 32

Look at the three pictures.
Write the story shown in the pictures.
Write **35 words** or more.

Write the story on your answer sheet.

LISTENING (approximately 30 minutes)

PART 1

QUESTIONS 1–5

For each question, choose the correct answer.

1   Where will the friends meet tonight?

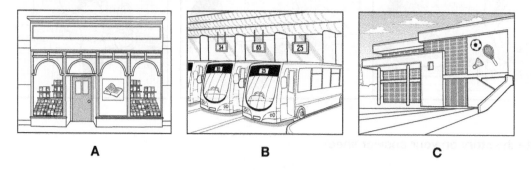

A   B   C

2   What did Sally eat at the restaurant?

A   B   C

3   What job is Tom's sister doing this summer?

A   B   C

4 What exercise is the woman going to do now?

A   **B**   **C**

5 What's Philip wearing?

A   **B**   **C**

PART 2

QUESTIONS 6–10

For each question, write the correct answer in the gap.
Write **one word** or a **number** or a **date** or a **time**.

___

You will hear Maria leaving a message for Bill with details of Tom's birthday party.

Tom's birthday party

Day: Saturday

Time guests arrive: (6) .... p.m.

Address: (7) 26 .... Road

Food: (8) .... and cake

Type of music: (9) ....

Maria's phone number: (10) ....

PART 3

QUESTIONS 11–15

For each question, choose the correct answer.

You will hear Andy talking to his friend Sara about a walk.

11   Where do they agree to meet?

   A   at a car park

   B   at a playground

   C   at a bus stop

12   What does Andy say the weather will be like for the walk?

   A   sunny

   B   windy

   C   rainy

13   What will Sara bring?

   A   a map

   B   a backpack

   C   a drink

14   What does Andy think about the Bridge Café?

   A   The prices are low.

   B   Its food is good.

   C   It's easy to get to.

15   How does Sara feel about going on the walk?

   A   pleased to get lots of exercise

   B   interested to see the lovely views

   C   happy to spend time with her friend

PART 4

QUESTIONS 16–20

For each question, choose the correct answer.

---

16 You will hear two friends talking about exercise.
What do they agree?

   A Running's hard.

   B Walking's boring.

   C Cycling's dangerous.

17 You will hear a woman talking about jobs.
What did she want to be when she was younger?

   A an artist

   B a journalist

   C a cook

18 You will hear two friends talking about going out.
Where do they agree to go?

   A to a concert

   B to an exhibition

   C to a film

19 You will hear a woman talking to her friend about finding a new job.
Why does the woman want the job?

   A The work is interesting.

   B The people are nice.

   C The office is near her home.

20 You will hear a woman talking to her brother on the phone.
Why is the woman happy?

   A She met an old friend.

   B She got an exciting job.

   C She found a new place to live.

PART 5

QUESTIONS 21–25

For each question, choose the correct answer.

You will hear a husband and wife talking about the furniture they need for their new home. What do they need for each room?

Example:

0	dining room	**A**

Rooms				**Furniture**	
21	kitchen			**A**	armchair
				B	bookcase
22	living room			**C**	cupboard
23	bedroom			**D**	desk
				E	lamp
24	bathroom			**F**	mirror
25	garage			**G**	picture
				H	shelf

You now have 6 minutes to write your answers on the answer sheet.

Test 4

READING AND WRITING (60 minutes)

PART 1

QUESTIONS 1–6

For each question, choose the correct answer.

1

Harry,
We're out of milk.
We'll need some
tonight, so can you
stop somewhere
on your way home
from college?
Dinner is at 6.
Mum

A Harry's mother is finding out what Harry wants for dinner.

B Harry's mother is telling Harry not to be late home tonight.

C Harry's mother is asking Harry to buy something for her.

2

Sammy,
The movie at the film club
tonight is very popular.
So shall I see you at our
usual meeting place, but
a bit earlier?
Tom

What does Tom want to change?

A the time he'll meet Sammy

B the place where he'll meet Sammy

C the movie he and Sammy will see

3

NOTICES

Harwood College Picnic
Saturday 1 p.m.

Sports field (Gym if raining)
Harwood students – free
Guests – £5
Fantastic band!
Food included

A Everyone who comes to the picnic should bring some food.

B The picnic won't happen if the weather is bad.

C Some people who come to the picnic must pay.

4

To: Emily
From: Carol

I'm driving to college every day this term. If you can pay a bit for petrol, I'll take you too. Parking's free.

Carol wants Emily

A to share the cost of driving to college.

B to give her a lift to college some days.

C to help pay for parking at college.

5

City Station

Bad weather!

Trains working as usual

Be careful of ice on platforms

What is the problem today?

A Trains might be late.

B Passengers might fall.

C The station might need to close.

6

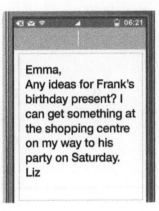

06:21

Emma,
Any ideas for Frank's birthday present? I can get something at the shopping centre on my way to his party on Saturday.
Liz

What is Liz doing in this text message?

A asking Emma to buy something

B asking Emma for some advice

C asking Emma to a party

PART 2

QUESTIONS 7–13

For each question, choose the correct answer.

		Eugenia	Laura	Ellie
7	Who thinks not enough music is taught in schools?	A	B	C
8	Who grew up in a home without much classical music?	A	B	C
9	Who likes to share ideas about music with people online?	A	B	C
10	Who says she thinks people should go to concerts?	A	B	C
11	Who started learning to play an instrument after she was given one?	A	B	C
12	Who is now studying music at university?	A	B	C
13	Who says her parents were surprised when she won a competition?	A	B	C

Future stars of classical music

Eugenia

My mother and father both play the violin in an orchestra, so that's what they began teaching me to play, even before I went to school. Now I've finished university and I'm a member of the same orchestra. I believe it's important for everyone to go to see music being played. Tickets are expensive, but it's a much better experience than just listening to recorded music. Over the years, I've won a few violin competitions and I love making music with my friends.

Laura

When I was a child, my father had a café and the only music there, and in our house, was jazz on the radio. But when I was 12, I went on a school trip and heard classical guitar for the first time. I loved it, and my mother bought me a guitar and paid for lessons. My parents couldn't believe it when I came first in a national guitar competition. I've left university now, but I'm still learning new things every day. There's so much information online.

Ellie

I'm now playing in my university orchestra and taking classes there in writing music, which is what I want to do as a career. I love using the internet to discuss things I'm working on with other musicians. I was lucky to be able to have classical violin lessons at school and, by the time I was eight, I was in the children's orchestra and playing in local competitions. In my opinion, more schools should offer music lessons. Music is so important.

PART 3

QUESTIONS 14–18

For each question, choose the correct answer.

A lucky teenager

Fifteen-year-old British student Jonathan Davis has always loved learning about the past. So, when he saw a newspaper article about people who enjoy looking in the countryside for very old things made of metal, such as coins, he wanted to try the hobby himself.

To get started, he had to have something called a detector. You hold this machine over the ground, and it makes a loud noise if there is metal there. He bought a small one and began using it near the village where he lives.

He didn't find much for the first few months. Then, one day, he and a friend were looking in a field. 'We were a bit bored,' he says. 'But suddenly, I found a few bits of metal lying in the grass. As soon as I saw them, I had a feeling they might be really old, so I showed them to my friend. We kept looking, and together we found 200 more pieces that day!'

Jonathan took the pieces to a museum. The staff there told him they were almost two thousand years old. They explained that at that time people sometimes cut silver bowls and cups into small pieces, and then used the pieces as money.

The museum later had a special exhibition of the silver pieces, which Jonathan went to. He said, 'It was really exciting to see what the people at the museum were able to do to clean the pieces of silver and find out exactly what they are. They look really different now. I'm so pleased I found them and that now other people can see them too.'

---

14   What do we learn about Jonathan from the first paragraph?

   A   He's interested in history.

   B   He has lots of unusual hobbies.

   C   He enjoys collecting old things.

15   What is the writer doing in the second paragraph?

   A   giving information about a village

   B   saying how some equipment works

   C   describing a problem Jonathan had

16   What does Jonathan say in the third paragraph about the metal pieces?

   A   He thought they looked interesting.

   B   It took several days to find all of them.

   C   He was pleased when his friend found them.

17   What did the staff at the museum tell Jonathan about the metal pieces?

   A   They were not as old as Jonathan thought.

   B   It's a shame they were so small.

   C   In the past, people used them to buy and sell things.

18   How did Jonathan feel when he visited the exhibition?

   A   surprised so many people came to see the silver

   B   happy he could share the silver with others

   C   sad that the silver looked so different

PART 4

QUESTIONS 19–24

For each question, choose the correct answer.

Toni Morrison

The African-American writer Toni Morrison was born in 1931. When she was growing up, her parents **(19)** .... her about African-American history and music. She often said that **(20)** .... stories was an important **(21)** .... of her family's daily life. She also loved books and spent a lot of her free time reading.

In 1949, Toni Morrison went to Howard University in Washington, D.C. to study English. After **(22)** .... her course, her first job was teaching. She wrote her first book, *The Bluest Eye*, in 1970. Her later books were very popular, **(23)** .... *Beloved*, which is now a well-known film. Toni Morrison **(24)** .... many national and international prizes, including the Nobel Prize for Literature in 1993. She became the first black woman ever to receive this.

---

19   **A**   learned   **B**   studied   **C**   taught

20   **A**   telling   **B**   saying   **C**   talking

21   **A**   thing   **B**   piece   **C**   part

22   **A**   closing   **B**   finishing   **C**   returning

23   **A**   usually   **B**   really   **C**   especially

24   **A**   won   **B**   made   **C**   took

PART 5

QUESTIONS 25–30

For each question, write the correct answer.
Write **ONE** word for each gap.

Example:	0	*to*

From: Marcia

To: Annie

I am trying **(0)** .... start a girls' basketball team at college. Are you interested

(25) .... joining it? Basketball's **(26)** .... excellent way to get exercise, and

it can also be a **(27)** .... of fun.

Our sports teacher, Mrs Thompson, says she will be our coach, but only **(28)** .... we can

get enough girls for a team. We will probably practise once or twice a week in the college gym.

(29) .... you know any other girls we can ask to be on the team? Let me know as soon

(30) .... possible so we can begin practising.

PART 6

QUESTION 31

You would like to go to the countryside this weekend.
Write an email to your English friend, Jerry.

In your email:

• ask Jerry to go with you

• tell Jerry what activities you'll do

• say who else you've asked to come.

Write **25 words** or more.

PART 7

QUESTION 32

Look at the three pictures.
Write the story shown in the pictures.
Write **35 words** or more.

Write the story on your answer sheet.

LISTENING (approximately 30 minutes)

PART 1

QUESTIONS 1–5

For each question, choose the correct answer.

---

1 What has Paul bought Timothy for his birthday?

A

B

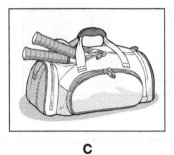
C

2 Where did John go last weekend?

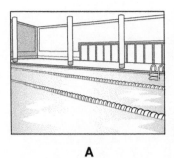
A

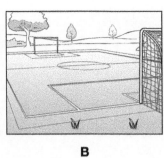
B

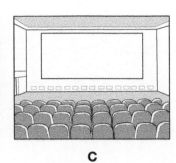
C

3 Where's Sally now?

A

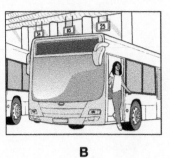
B

C

4 Which sport is the woman going to do at the sports centre?

A   B   C

5 What has the woman bought for her new apartment?

A   B   C

PART 2

QUESTIONS 6–10

For each question, write the correct answer in the gap.
Write **one word** or a **number** or a **date** or a **time**.

You will hear a coach driver telling tourists about their visit to an animal park.

Langate Animal Park

Remember to take: umbrellas

Type of animal Langate is famous for: (6) ....

Good place to take photos: (7) ....

Start time of guide's talk: (8) .... a.m.

Cost of lunch: (9) £...

Wait for coach at entrance called: (10) ....

PART 3

QUESTIONS 11–15

For each question, choose the correct answer.

You will hear two friends, Sophie and John, talking about planning a picnic that they have every year with neighbours.

11 What does Sophie like most about the picnic?

    A   eating great food

    B   spending time outdoors

    C   becoming better friends with people

12 Where is the picnic going to be this year?

    A   a park

    B   a lake

    C   a garden

13 What happened at last year's picnic?

    A   The weather wasn't very good.

    B   Some people didn't enjoy themselves.

    C   Some people didn't know where to go.

14 What does Sophie want guests to bring?

    A   something to do

    B   something to eat with

    C   something to barbecue

15 Which job does John say he'll do?

    A   speak to people

    B   put signs in the area

    C   send a group email

PART 4

QUESTIONS 16–20

For each question, choose the correct answer.

---

16 You will hear a woman giving a talk.
What's the woman's job?

   A   engineer

   B   farmer

   C   painter

17 You will hear a man talking to his sister about a new friend.
Where did the man meet his new friend?

   A   at work

   B   at a party

   C   at a sports match

18 You will hear a husband and wife talking about going to the cinema.
Why do they decide to walk to the cinema?

   A   There are no buses today.

   B   They want some exercise.

   C   The car isn't working.

19 You will hear a man telling a woman about his holiday.
What problem did he have on the holiday?

   A   The weather was bad.

   B   The beach was dirty.

   C   The hotel was noisy.

20 You will hear a girl talking with her dad about learning a new language.
What did the girl like about her first Chinese lesson?

   A   the other students

   B   the teacher

   C   the length of the lesson

PART 5

QUESTIONS 21–25

For each question, choose the correct answer.

You will hear two friends talking about a party on the beach.
What will each person bring to the party?

Example:

0	Ben	C

People			**Things to bring**	
21	Katy		**A**	beach umbrella
22	Jacob		**B**	blanket
23	Suzana		**C**	football
24	Martin		**D**	games
25	Carla		**E**	photos
			F	picnic
			G	sunglasses
			H	towels

You now have 6 minutes to write your answers on the answer sheet.

Sample answer sheet: Reading and Writing

Cambridge Assessment
English

Candidate Name	
Centre Name	
Examination Title	

Candidate Number	
Centre Number	
Examination Details	
Assessment Date	

Candidate Signature

Supervisor: If the candidate is ABSENT or has WITHDRAWN shade here ○

Key Reading and Writing Candidate Answer Sheet

Instructions
Use a PENCIL (B or HB).
Rub out any answer you want to change with an eraser.

For Parts 1, 2, 3 and 4:
Mark ONE letter for each answer.
For example: If you think A is the right answer to the question, mark your answer sheet like this:

For Part 5:
Write your answers clearly in the spaces next to the numbers (25 to 30) like this:

0 | E N G L I S H

Write your answers in CAPITAL LETTERS.

Part 1

	A	B	C
1	○	○	○
2	○	○	○
3	○	○	○
4	○	○	○
5	○	○	○
6	○	○	○

Part 2

	A	B	C
7	○	○	○
8	○	○	○
9	○	○	○
10	○	○	○
11	○	○	○
12	○	○	○
13	○	○	○

Part 3

	A	B	C
14	○	○	○
15	○	○	○
16	○	○	○
17	○	○	○
18	○	○	○

Part 4

	A	B	C
19	○	○	○
20	○	○	○
21	○	○	○
22	○	○	○
23	○	○	○
24	○	○	○

Part 5

		Do not write below here			Do not write below here
25		25 1 ○ 0 ○	28		28 1 ○ 0 ○
26		26 1 ○ 0 ○	29		29 1 ○ 0 ○
27		27 1 ○ 0 ○	30		30 1 ○ 0 ○

Put your answers to Writing Parts 6 and 7 on the separate Answer Sheet

OFFICE USE ONLY - DO NOT WRITE OR MAKE ANY MARK BELOW THIS LINE   Page 1 of 1

Draft

Draft

Cambridge Assessment
English

Candidate Name

Candidate Number

Centre Name

Centre Number

Examination Title

Examination Details

Candidate Signature

Assessment Date

Supervisor: If the candidate is ABSENT or has WITHDRAWN shade here ○

Key Writing

Candidate Answer Sheet for Parts 6 and 7

INSTRUCTIONS TO CANDIDATES

Make sure that your name and candidate number are on this sheet.

Write your answers to Writing Parts 6 and 7 on the other side of this sheet.

Use a pencil.

You **must** write within the grey lines.

Do **not** write on the bar codes.

Draft

Sample answer sheet: Reading and Writing

Part 6: Write your answer below.

Part 7: Write your answer below.

Examiner's Use Only

Part 6	C	O	L

Part 7	C	O	L

© Cambridge Assessment 2020

Draft

Page 1 of 1

Cambridge Assessment
English

Candidate Name		Candidate Number	
Centre Name		Centre Number	
Examination Title		Examination Details	
Candidate Signature		Assessment Date	

Supervisor: If the candidate is ABSENT or has WITHDRAWN shade here ○

Key Listening Candidate Answer Sheet

Instructions
Use a PENCIL (B or HB).
Rub out any answer you want to change with an eraser.

For Parts 1, 3, 4 and 5:
Mark ONE letter for each answer.
For example: If you think A is the right answer to the question, mark your answer sheet like this: 0 A ● B ○ C ○

For Part 2:
Write your answers clearly in the spaces next to the numbers (6 to 10) like this:

0 | E N G L I S H

Write your answers in CAPITAL LETTERS.

Part 1
1 A ○ B ○ C ○
2 A ○ B ○ C ○
3 A ○ B ○ C ○
4 A ○ B ○ C ○
5 A ○ B ○ C ○

Part 2
6 _____
7 _____
8 _____
9 _____
10 _____

Do not write below here
6 | 1 ○ 0 ○
7 | 1 ○ 0 ○
8 | 1 ○ 0 ○
9 | 1 ○ 0 ○
10 | 1 ○ 0 ○

Part 3
11 A ○ B ○ C ○
12 A ○ B ○ C ○
13 A ○ B ○ C ○
14 A ○ B ○ C ○
15 A ○ B ○ C ○

Part 4
16 A ○ B ○ C ○
17 A ○ B ○ C ○
18 A ○ B ○ C ○
19 A ○ B ○ C ○
20 A ○ B ○ C ○

Part 5
21 A ○ B ○ C ○ D ○ E ○ F ○ G ○ H ○
22 A ○ B ○ C ○ D ○ E ○ F ○ G ○ H ○
23 A ○ B ○ C ○ D ○ E ○ F ○ G ○ H ○
24 A ○ B ○ C ○ D ○ E ○ F ○ G ○ H ○
25 A ○ B ○ C ○ D ○ E ○ F ○ G ○ H ○

Page 1 of 1

Draft

Acknowledgements

The authors and publishers acknowledge the following sources of copyright material and are grateful for the permissions granted. While every effort has been made, it has not always been possible to identify the sources of all the material used, or to trace all copyright holders. If any omissions are brought to our notice, we will be happy to include the appropriate acknowledgements on reprinting and in the next update to the digital edition, as applicable.

Key: T = Test, RW = Reading & Writing

Photography

All the photographs are sourced from Getty Images.

T1 RW: Sarah Casillas/DigitalVision; monkeybusinessimages/iStock/Getty Images Plus; Ben Gingell/iStock/Getty Images Plus;
T2 RW: monkeybusinessimages/iStock/Getty Images Plus; Ishii Koji/DigitalVision; Image Source/DigitalVision;
T4 RW: Maskot; Steve Debenport/E+; gustavofrazao/iStock/Getty Images Plus.

Illustrations commissioned by Cambridge Assessment.

Typeset by QBS Learning.

Audio production by Real Deal Productions and dsound recording Ltd.

Visual materials for the Speaking test

Test 1
Do you like these different sports?

Test 2
Do you like these different hobbies?

Test 3

Do you like these different ways of travelling in a city?

Test 4
Do you like these different activities to do in the countryside?